Thinking About Homeschool?

"What About Science/Math?"

Learning to learn with each other

Written by Robin and Tony Weaver

Art by Polina Hrytskova

Inspirational credits to The Hill Country Homeschoolers and Golden Eagle Charter School, Sweet Berry Farm and Hunter Orchards, Harmony School for the Arts and Mount Shasta Art Bus, Mount Shasta Martial Arts Program and AcroTex Gymnastics, YMCA and Mount Shasta Fitness Center, US Forest Service and State Parks, Botanical Gardens and City Parks, Safaris and Zoos, Museums, Universities, Family, Friends, Neighbors ......

Habitats & Homesteads

Thinking About Homeschool?
What About Science/Math?

Copyright 2018 © by

Habitats and Homesteads, LLC
507 Mill Street
Mount Shasta, CA 96067
USA
habitatsandhomesteads.com

Written by
Tony, Robin, Lily, Elder Weaver

Art by
Polina Hrytskova

Habitats & Homesteads

What About Science/Math?

Catrina figures it out!

Wow! That is one big creature. I wonder what it was like when the dinosaurs were around? This museum has me curious about so many things. When I get home, I am going to read about all of them.

I talk with my mama and papa about all the things I want to learn. Dinosaurs are only one thing I like to study. My parents help me decide what materials I need to explore all my interests

My parents are finally getting me a microscope. I have really wanted one for a long time. I will be able to look at all the tiny things that I find.

Today, Papa is helping me build a model rocket. I love learning with him because he knows a lot about outer space.

My papa helped us start a model rocket club.
We are at a safe place and I'm checking the wind to
make sure that it's ok for us to launch our rockets.
It is safe because there's only a light breeze.

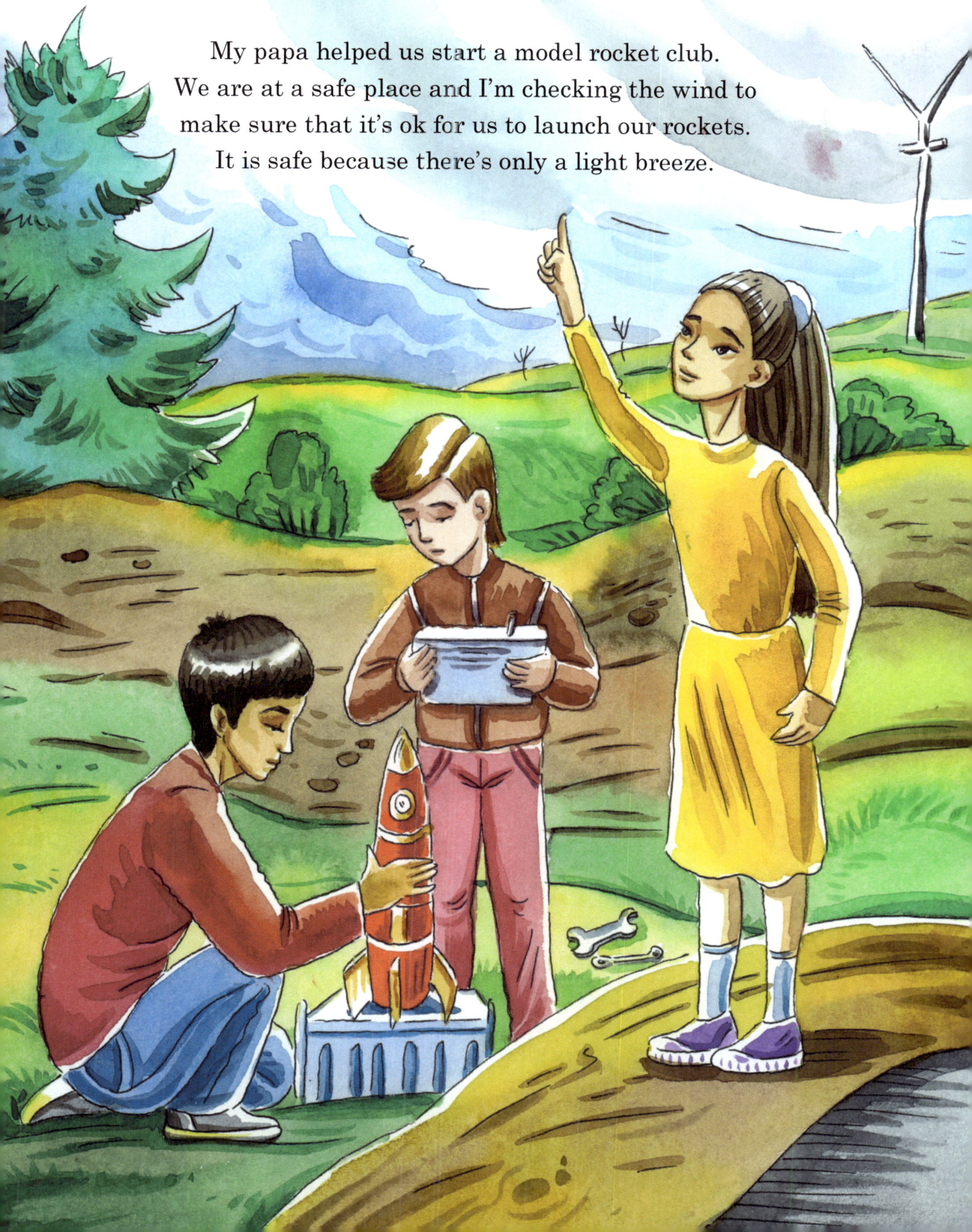

At park day, my friend Hannah is helping me catch bugs to look at with my new microscope. We are finding mostly ants and slimy worms. I am also collecting some tiny leaves and flowers.

My mama wants me to start making dinner for the family once a week. I have to think of a healthy meal and find a recipe, then my brother Philip will take me to the store to buy the ingredients.

Everyone in my family likes pizza, so I am making some. I'm teaching myself how to measure the ingredients with special spoons and cups.

CORNMAZE

Some of us kids in the homeschool science class built a pumpkin shooter at the Homeschool Harvest Festival. We are raising money for a big field trip by charging $5.00 to shoot each pumpkin.

It's getting cold outside and the birds are flying south for the winter. I like to see them up close with my binoculars so I can identify each kind of bird. It's amazing that they can fly so far. I wish I could fly.

My friends and I are learning about how coffee is made. We are looking at a big machine that roasts coffee beans up to 530 degrees. That's really hot! I didn't know that Mama drank beans in the morning.

My Mama's family is coming to visit during the holidays, so we are putting up a lot of decorations. I'm testing the lights and finding all the bulbs that are burned out so I can fix them and learn about electricity.

Today I'm making electricity with a lemon. It's called a circuit! I think it's amazing how many things you can learn on the internet.

My friends call me the Official Snowball Maker at winter park days.
My mama taught me how to make them all perfect spheres.
They look just like baseballs.

I am building a bridge out of toothpicks for the homeschool science class this month. It takes a long time because the glue has to dry. I made a bunch of triangles first and then put them all together. Triangles are the strongest shape.

I love our homeschool science class. We are adding sand to a bucket to test how much weight our bridges can hold. Orlando's bridge held 17 pounds before it broke! Now we are testing mine...

I wrote a report about Madame Curie for Book Club. She was a really famous woman scientist. We are all learning about historical people that we like at the library.

I know all kinds of things about volcanoes. I'm showing my friends the one
I made that explodes using baking soda and vinegar.
We are all planning to take a hike to a real volcano next week.

Today we are going to a State Park to hike on a volcano.
I am showing the other kids how I learned to use a
compass and map so we don't get lost.

Willow needs help up some of the steep parts on our hike. She is telling me all the names of the wildflowers. I am telling her all about how these mountains and rivers are formed.

We are finally here! A lot of homeschool families go camping on the beach every year. It's really fun running away from the waves but sometimes the powerful tide catches us and knocks us over.
I can't stop laughing!

We are using the money from the pumpkin shooter at the Home School Harvest Festival to visit an aquarium by the ocean. Jack and I both really like watching the jellyfish that glow in the dark.

My online math program is teaching me about graphs. I decided to practice making a graph at the lake by recording who could skip a rock the farthest and the most times.

Every spring all of us kids pick up trash at some of our favorite places.
I am collecting water at the river to look at with my microscope.
It is important to keep our water clean and safe.

It is incredible how many tiny creatures are swimming around with us in our river water. All of them are safe ones so far. I want to identify everything that I find!

It is time to plant the spring garden. I am measuring how far apart to plant all the vegetables and herbs. We need to make sure that all the different sized plants have enough room to grow.

After learning about worm composting at the garden, I decided to cut one open to look at it's digestive system. Worms eat our compost to help feed the growing plants.

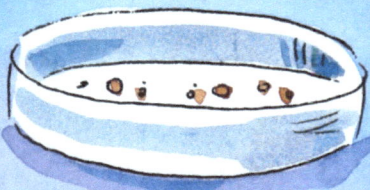

My family is going on a really fun trip. I'm excited while I'm packing up to go on another adventure. I already packed my science gear and almost forgot about my clothes! I hope there is enough room in the car for everything.

I'm so lucky! My parents brought me to Space Camp! I've already
learned about all the planets in our solar system but now I am going
to study the whole universe. I can't wait to learn about different stars,
black holes, the International Space Station, talk to astronauts and...

www.ingramcontent.com/pod-product-compliance
Lightning Source LLC
Chambersburg PA
CBHW042056040426
42447CB00003B/247